BOUNDARY SETTING

ALSO BY REV. DR. JIM STOUT

All books are (or soon will be) available online through Amazon and other stores in both printed and e-book formats. They can be purchased or ordered at many local bookstores as well. Further information can be found by visiting Dr. Stout's website, www.drjimstout.com.

Please consider purchasing some of these life-enhancing publications for yourself, or as gifts for family members, friends, patients, clergy, or mental-medical health providers. They are ideal for encouragement gifts, bulk orders, special promotions, and other uses. A portion of the profits from these will be used for various mental illness, clergy, and career-guidance ministries.

BIPOLAR DISORDER—REBUILDING YOUR LIFE: *A Bipolar's Story That Includes Practical Strategies, Techniques, and Tips for Managing Moods* — Rev. Dr. Jim Stout's popular autobiographical self-help book for patients, family members, and mental-medical health professionals

RECOVERING AND REBUILDING FROM A SEVERE MENTAL ILLNESS
Rev. Dr. Jim Stout's story, which includes concrete recovery strategies for strugglers

BOUNDARY SETTING FOR CLERGY AND MINISTRY WORKERS
Protect your ministry and minimize stress

ABANDONED AND BETRAYED BY GOD: *Surviving a Crisis of Faith*
For those dealing with adversities and faith issues

MENTAL ILLNESS AND YOUR MARRIAGE: *Surviving, Coping, Healing, and Rebuilding* — Candid sharing and useful strategies for repairing and enriching your marriage

SHATTERED DREAMS: *How to Overcome Unmet Expectations* Positive guides for the disappointed or distressed

STRESS BUSTING — Includes user-friendly approaches for avoiding unnecessary pressures, as well as tips for coping with stress-causing people and situations

BEATING DEPRESSION: *Surviving, Coping, Healing, and Rebuilding* Provides valuable tools, both for recovering from serious depression and for helping a depressed loved one

WRITINGS OF PAIN, WRITINGS OF HOPE: *Reflections from a Journey Through Severe Depression* — Understand the way a depressed person thinks

CHANGING GEARS: *Making the Most of the Second Half of Your Life* — Real-world actions for reinventing yourself and getting the most from your coming years

AN EMERGENCY GUIDE TO DEPRESSION AND BIPOLAR DISORDER: *How to Survive a Crisis* — Proven methods for managing critical situations

REBOUNDING: *How to Find Your Purpose in Life Despite Your Losses* — Workable ways for getting unstuck and moving ahead with your life

BUILDING A STRONGER MARRIAGE AND FAMILY: *A Helpful Guide to Mending and Enhancing Your Home Life* — Down-to-earth strategies for strengthening your marriage and parenting skills

BOUNDARY SETTING

A Practical Guide

REV. DR. JIM STOUT

SHEPHERD PUBLISHING

The information in this book is intended to complement, not substitute for, the advice of your physician, psychiatrist, psychologist, MFT, MSW, or other mental-medical health provider. Please consult him or her about your unique needs. If you are in urgent difficulty, phone 911 or a crisis hotline, such as the National Suicide Prevention Crisis Hotline at 1-800-273-TALK (1-800-273-8255).

Edited by Andrew Kroeger and Stephanie Starr. Cover design by Andrew Kroeger.

Cover photo from iStock.

ISBN: 978-1-942648-40-6

DEDICATED WITH GRATITUDE

To the many clergy, Young Life staff, psychologists, Gordon-Conwell and Fuller Seminary professors, and friends who have modeled healthy boundaries that have encouraged and inspired me.

To our sons, John and Jim, Jr., who have modeled boundary setting and taught me and others by their examples.

To my wife Leah, above all, for her patience, prayers, and unconditional love in my boundary-setting successes and failures.

AUTHOR'S NOTES

For the reader's convenience, and for clarification, I have:

- used the *New International Version* for all Bible verses, added reference endnotes with verse location, and italicized all verses;
- chosen to refer to God with male pronouns (he, him, his). Gender equality is important to me in all areas, including language about God, whom I believe has strong female characteristics as well as male ones. The Scriptures certainly refer to God's female attributes as well as male ones. However, for simplicity's sake, I have chosen to refer to God as a male;
- used either *he* or *she* rather than the longer *he and/or she* for brevity when referring to men or women. In most cases, *he* or *she* is intended to refer to anyone, regardless of gender; and
- changed certain names in order to protect an individual's privacy.

I applied my heart to what I observed and
learned a lesson from what I saw.

Proverbs 24:32

CONTENTS

INTRODUCTION

BY ALL RIGHTS, MY MINISTRY, MARRIAGE, AND FAMILY LIFE should have been shipwrecked forty years ago due to the consequences of my boundary ignorance, denial, and poor maintenance. Yet by a series of miracles, my work and home life were spared.

I'd logged in more than twenty years of counseling with clergy and ministry workers who were facing serious boundary-related difficulties before I'd actually heard of the term *boundaries*. It was used by Dr. John Townsend and Dr. Henry Cloud, who were teaching on the subject. Their words opened my eyes to the importance of creating and enforcing boundaries at work, home, and in one's personal life.

Since then, dozens of helpful books about boundaries have been published. To better equip myself, I've read voraciously on boundary issues, and I've conferred with many counselors on boundary topics.

Throughout this time, I realized I was not alone in my boundary struggles. Countless men, women, and youth live with increasing boundary-related stress, depression, and burnout, as well as personal and family problems. And it is getting worse.

Many people live without clear personal or professional boundaries. Often, the boundaries they do have are weak or unenforced. They work under constant stress, trapped with feelings of guilt, anger, resentment, fear, and depression. Their boundary inadequacies rob them of healthy self-confidence and inner peace.

Along with numerous counseling experts, I believe that setting and maintaining boundaries is the *key* to a fulfilling personal life and successful ministry.

What about you? If you picked up this book, chances are you are facing your own boundary challenges.

Want to experience emotional relief from the frustrations, resentments, and anxieties that come from a lack of good boundaries?

The purpose of this book is to share some of the lessons on setting and maintaining boundaries that I, and many of my colleagues, have learned from the trenches in our work, home, and personal lives—what has and hasn't worked.

This book will help you discover five things about boundaries:

1. Common boundary issues to look out for
2. Collateral damages that these boundary issues create
3. Proactive ways to avoid, cope with, or overcome conflicts by setting and maintaining good boundaries
4. Concrete actions you can take to minimize the negative effects of non-existent or weak boundaries
5. Practical guidelines for starting, strengthening, or maintaining your boundaries

Besides merely knowing academic facts about the relentless pressures of boundary conflicts, I also bear the scars from my own failures with them.

This book doesn't claim to be the last word on boundaries—it's simply my attempt to pass on what I, and others, have learned through our boundary successes and failures.

When sharing with you in the pages ahead, my approach is similar to D. T. Niles's description of evangelism: "One beggar sharing with another beggar where to find bread."

As you read through this discussion, please apply the oft-used slogan from Alcoholics Anonymous: "Take what works and leave the rest."

With this in mind, I hope this book will generate a huge payoff for you in every area of your life. Let's begin.

CHAPTER 1

The Number One Killer

PROFESSIONALS SAY, HANDS DOWN, THAT THE BIGGEST CAREER, marriage, and family killer—regardless of age, socioeconomic status, education, or faith—is a lack of strong, clear boundaries.

My own experience as a pastor, and as one who has counseled countless men and women, underlines the critical importance of creating and enforcing boundaries in one's work and personal life.

The key boundary-struggle areas for most people revolve around:

- work areas, such as job description, work hours, staff issues, and expectations that others have for you and your work; and
- non-work areas, such as marriage, parenting, relatives, personal finances, and social obligations.

A JOB CAN BE A FRIENDLY MONSTER

Work can eat away at your personal and family time so subtly that you barely notice its effects until it's too late and you have no life apart from your job.

Slowly but surely, your whole existence is taken over by your career, at the cost of neglecting your loved ones and yourself.

PGA (Professional Golfers' Association) caddie John "Cubby" Burke made a shrewd observation about how golf hooks many pro golfers. He said that after a while they come "under the influence of golf." By this, he meant that their obsession with golf ends up being the only thing left in their lives.

In similar ways, workplaces, marriages, and families are tragically littered with the skeletal remains of individuals who didn't set good boundaries and simply couldn't say no. Unfortunately, they sacrificed their family life and personal time to do whatever it took to "become all things to all people."

Recently, I saw a T-shirt that perfectly describes the life of a vast number of people:

> LET ME DROP EVERYTHING
> & WORK ON YOUR PROBLEM!

During the first twenty years of my ministry, I worked an average of more than seventy hours a week. It was a hectic schedule jammed with meetings, counseling, preaching, speaking, staff issues, hospital visitations, weddings, funerals, and a slew of other responsibilities. There was little time left over for my family, let alone my own needs.

I certainly echo the sad truth that a Christian college professor lamented to his class: "Busyness is the only sin that is *applauded* by the Church!" I don't know if you've ever been praised for your long work hours, but I have. Sadly, this motivated me to work even more.

BOUNDARIES IN THE BIBLE

Boundaries, both physical and emotional, play key roles in the Bible. For example, the Lord said to Moses:

> *Command the Israelites and say to them: "When you enter Canaan, the land that will be allotted to you as an inheritance is to have these boundaries" . . . This will be your land, with its boundaries on every side.* [1]

Remember the parable of the Good Samaritan who helped an injured man who'd been robbed and beaten? This story is a great illustration of boundary setting.

The traveling Samaritan came upon an injured man. He could have gone on, but he stopped, applied first aid, and paid for the man's recovery. Then he took the fellow to a local inn and left him in the care of the innkeeper, promising to pay any future expenses. But the Samaritan didn't allow this to delay his trip. While he chose to allow an unexpected interruption, he guarded his time and stayed on schedule. He maintained boundaries that limited *how* he used his time.

Jesus clearly used boundaries in his life and ministry. Whereas many people are tempted to please everyone, Jesus stuck to his limits and didn't try to meet everyone's needs or agendas. For example, even when facing multitudes of people needing his help, Jesus took time off for strategic rest and prayer:

> *Yet the news about him spread all the more, so that crowds of people came to hear him and to be healed*

of their sicknesses. But Jesus often withdrew to lonely places and prayed. [2]

How often do you get away from your ministry pressures to find refreshment and renewal? In what ways can you do this in the midst of dealing with needy people and programs?

BOUNDARY PROBLEMS IN THE MODERN WORKPLACE

There is an interesting parallel between professional football and full-time work. Like other large corporations, the NFL (National Football League) is a big-time profit machine. The sole, driving purpose of its coaches and office staff is to win football games. To do this, some teams' management will ignore a player's injuries and long-term health. They will use players until they are absolutely drained or are severely, sometimes irreparably, injured.

Unfortunately, like the NFL, many companies and organizations also exploit their leaders and staff, saddling them with unrealistic demands that disregard their personal well-being.

However, we can't totally blame our management—oftentimes the villain in our workplace is *us*. We can be our own worst enemy when it comes to our priorities and time use.

DEALING WITH A "MESSIAH COMPLEX"

Many people live with a "Messiah Complex," believing they are the single most important link in the chain of their job's effectiveness. Sure, intellectually they believe God will take care of everything. But in practice, they act as though their company's or organization's success depends primarily on *their* personal actions. Despite their biblical beliefs, their actions flesh out, "If *I* don't do it, it won't get done."

I labored under this Messiah Complex for a long time. Now I can joke about my foolishness:

> **Question:** Do you know what the difference is between God and Jim Stout?
> **Answer:** God doesn't think he's Jim Stout!

With such hectic schedules, it's no wonder that individuals "grow weary in well-doing" and experience burnout. How about you? Do you feel overworked or overcommitted?

CHAPTER 2

Types of Boundary Problems

HOW IS IT POSSIBLE TO BUILD A HAPPY, BALANCED HOME life when you are always gone? If you say yes to too many work-related requests, your family and personal life will suffer.

Obviously, some hard questions need to be raised: What does your job description say about your overtime work? Do you have the courage to bring up with your supervisor the tension between your job description's use of time and your *actual* use of time? What kind of boundaries can you set to protect yourself from exceeding reasonable work hours?

What is meant by a "boundary"? *Webster's New World Dictionary* defines it as, "Any line or thing marking a limit." [1]

It is also important to clarify the difference between a goal and a boundary. A goal describes a desired accomplishment. A boundary is a limit—a barrier that is used to protect, improve, or enhance goals. Clear, firm, and enforced boundaries are critical prerequisites for goal achievement, whether in work, personal, or family areas.

BOUNDARY TYPES

Most boundaries are physical or emotional. They mark what you will and will not tolerate from others. They also serve to protect you from your own potentially destructive words or actions.

Physical boundaries can be barriers like fences, walls, hedges, doors, and gates. They are used to keep people and things in or out—such as thieves, bad weather, pets, or insects.

But physical boundaries also include limits on work or other activities. This can mean abiding by written or verbal contracts, or avoiding situations that can physically hurt you or others, like reckless driving or physical abuse. Good physical boundaries can also be applied to control job descriptions, days off, exercise times, or even time limits for phone calls.

Emotional boundaries are usually used to manage the harmful words and deeds of others. These boundaries often limit their verbal abuse like shouting, threatening, cursing, belittling, or bullying.

Emotional boundaries can also apply to you, personally, when your own words or actions could have harmful effects on you, your family, or others. Self-set emotional boundaries can include taking a walk before you explode in anger, making time for regular peer support, going on a vacation when you're feeling overwhelmed at work, getting therapy for yourself, or limiting your own negative self-talk.

EXAMPLES OF COMMON BOUNDARY ISSUES

Can you relate to any of the following common boundary collisions? Each situation requires making a choice to either surrender your boundary limit or maintain it. How would you respond to these real-life circumstances?

Phone Calls During Mealtimes

The phone rings and you hear a non-urgent voice message. Do you take the call and interrupt your family time or a social event with friends? Or do you observe your "no-phone-call-interruptions-at-mealtimes" boundary and return the call later?

Verbal Abuse from Toxic People

A family member or coworker has another temper explosion and starts raising his voice at you with all kinds of accusations and putdowns. Do you silently take the criticisms? Or do you stand up for yourself and say, "I'm sorry you're so upset, but I won't tolerate you talking this way. If you continue, I'll walk out of the room. When you're able to cool down, call me and we'll talk again"?

You are invited to a Thanksgiving dinner with your relatives. One uncle has always been toxic toward you by repeatedly criticizing your occupation. Do you decline the invitation? Or do you accept the offer and risk more verbal arrows? If that uncle starts up his criticisms, do you have the courage to say, "I'm sorry you disagree with my career choice, but I refuse to listen to any more of your unjust criticisms. If you continue, I'll leave"?

Violations of Days Off

Saturdays and Sundays are your days off. You receive a call from a neighbor asking you to visit another neighbor who's been hospitalized for a non-emergency problem. Do you interrupt your family time? Or do you say, "Thanks for letting me know this. I have other commitments today, but I will see her later this week"?

You are invited to a coworker's 60th birthday party on your day off. Do you agree to attend? Or do you say, "I'd love to, but I can't"?

Violations of Evenings Off

You have saved Thursday evenings for a family movie night. You get a call from your boss requesting that you attend a last-minute meeting. As you listen, it's clear that this really isn't a critical situation that truly needs your immediate presence. Do you give in and rush out to the meeting?

Or do you silently reason with yourself that if your boss had a non-emergency on a Thursday evening and called a plumber, electrician, or doctor, wouldn't that professional ask him to call for a regular daytime appointment? Would you then say, "I'm sorry for your difficulty, but I've got a commitment this evening and can't discuss your issue right now. Please call me tomorrow and we'll set a time to talk"?

Due to evening meetings and other work-related responsibilities, you have only three nights a week at home. Inevitably, something goes wrong at work and you get called in to solve it. Soon, one or two more evenings are eaten up by overseeing these extra meetings, doing emergency "crisis repairs" at the office. Do you continue to let these "emergencies" steal your family time, or do you say, "I'm sorry, I already have a commitment with my family on those evenings."

Violations of Personal Limits

You have an established, three-afternoons-a-week routine at the gym. A friend wants you to skip a workout and go to a movie with him. Do you bend your exercise boundary? Or do you say, "No, thanks. I've got to stick to my exercise program"?

You've started a diet program. At lunch, a friend offers to buy you a piece of apple pie for dessert. Do you give in? Or do you stand up for your diet limits and say, "Thanks, but I've got to stick to my food plan"?

Your teenager asks for a loan to buy a stereo system. Do you respond, "Sure, here's the money. Pay it back whenever you can"? Or do you say, "Sure, but first let's write up an agreement on when and how you'll repay me"?

Violations of Professional or Moral Limits

Let's say you are a male business professional. You have plans to travel alone to a meeting an hour away, but then a woman from your office asks to carpool. Do you encourage her to go with someone else? Or do you take her with you?

A woman at work tends to hug you extra long, mixes her hugs with kisses, and makes suggestive comments. Do you back away and avoid future contact? Or do you rationalize that she is just needy and benefits from a physical connection?

A female coworker invites you to lunch to discuss a work project. Do you accept and sit in an open, visible place? Do you tell your wife or girlfriend ahead of time that you will be having lunch with another woman? Could you invite someone else to join the two of you?

Unclear Job Descriptions

You receive invitations to serve on various committees, boards, and task forces outside of your job. These might include a local hospital, little league, the Chamber of Commerce, Rotary, Red Cross, AIDS Foundation, homeless assistance, or domestic violence prevention. Each represents a worthy cause, but all are voluntary. Which should you choose? You can't do them all—something has to give. But where do you start cutting? What do you say to those who desperately insist on your help?

You are asked to take on an extra project at work. In addition to your current responsibilities, it will require working on Saturdays and one evening a week for the next six months. It will provide great financial benefits, but it will cut into valuable time with your teenage daughter, who is having a rough time with school and friends. If you decline, your boss may be upset with you. But what about the support your daughter desperately needs right now? What can you say to your supervisor that will enable you to address the needs of both your daughter and the extra project?

CHAPTER 3

Rationalizations for Poor Boundaries

IT'S EASY TO AVOID DEALING WITH A BOUNDARY PROBLEM by rationalizing, "My over-committed lifestyle won't last forever. Besides, things are going okay for me and my family. I'll slow down next month." Or the ever-popular: "Negative things won't happen to me, because I'm doing the best I can with long work hours and difficult people. Somehow, God will protect me and my family from my non-stop lifestyle."

Although aware that boundary issues are causing appalling problems, most men and women persist in their time-use struggles—unwilling or afraid to make necessary changes—hoping that someday, somehow, things will "work out."

This kind of reasoning is unrealistic. It denies past failures and ignores facts. This is why most 12-step groups call this warped perception "stinking thinking." Others refer to this twisted rationalizing as "insanity"—the act of "doing the same thing over and over, and each time expecting different results."

THE "MY JOB REQUIRES FULL DEDICATION" FALLACY

Vast numbers of people justify their boundary collapses by repeating the mantra: "My job requires full dedication. I must work extra-long hours and do time-consuming things to get ahead, or even to survive."

Last year, I came across a cartoon that showed a psychologist sitting next to his patient, who was slouched on the counseling couch. He had headphones over one ear and a computer on his lap as he busily listened to messages and typed at the same time. The psychologist asked, "When did you first suspect you were a workaholic?" Ouch—that could have described me for over twenty years!

THE DESIRE TO KEEP EVERYONE HAPPY

Whether in work or personal life, nearly everyone wants to be liked and respected, and some people go to great lengths to gain other people's esteem.

I know of one senior female executive from a large, long-established business who decided to organize a birthday party for every employee in her region, the anniversaries of all employees who celebrated fifty-year anniversaries, and attend all wedding and funeral receptions.

A huge chunk of her time was soon being taken up by these functions, leaving much less time for planning, board meetings, and key committees, not to mention her own family's activities. Obviously, she needed to review her priorities and set boundaries on the use of her time.

THE TEMPTATION TO WORK ON OTHER THINGS

For more than ten years, I've been working on several major book projects. It's been an ongoing battle to find time to write—nearly every week I've encountered enticing opportunities to work on other ventures, many of them worthy causes. Whenever I wandered off course to undertake a new project, I found that it siphoned off valuable time from my main endeavor: writing.

There will always be small and large temptations to divert your time and energy away from your important priorities. These time-robbers will never stop nibbling at your heels—you can count on it. So, remember to tell yourself, frequently:

- I can't do everything.
- I can never please everyone.
- There will always be unfinished tasks.

Like you, I know plenty of top-notch time management techniques and Bible verses. These were helpful in managing my priorities and my time, but they always fell short, at least until I took deliberate steps to set and maintain boundaries.

While I've come a long way, it's still a wrestling match. A phrase from Robert Frost's poem "Stopping by Woods on a Snowy Evening" has helped me in my effort:

> The woods are lovely, dark and deep,
> But I have promises to keep,
> And miles to go before I sleep,
> And miles to go before I sleep. [1]

Frost's words kept me on target to publish my first book, *Bipolar Disorder: Rebuilding Your Life*, and to finish a dozen more books since then.

CHAPTER 4

The Effects of Weak Boundaries

A LACK OF CLEAR PERSONAL OR PROFESSIONAL BOUNDARIES can lead to several types of serious difficulties.

UNHAPPY COWORKERS, UNHAPPY FAMILY

Let's face it: if you *don't* set and maintain boundaries, you *will* lose time and intimacy with your family. Yet when you *do* set limits, you may lose the approval of some coworkers. Either way, you can't win. When you are tempted to surrender your boundary limits to others' opinions, remind yourself of what you already know: by trying to please everyone, you please no one. Recently, I saw a sign that underscores this:

> I can only please one person per day.
> Today is not your day.
> Tomorrow doesn't look good either.

A hard fact of life is that you often must make tough, no-win choices. This truth certainly applies to boundary setting, both in your job and in your home life. Most working professionals face these choices weekly.

On one hand, if you cut out work opportunities and obligations, you will probably not accomplish some of the goals you've dreamed of for your career. On the other hand, if you do not preserve your personal and family time, those important parts of your life will suffer.

Boundary implementation and maintenance is crucial to keeping a proper balance. If you continue on a course of escalating your workload to fifty- or sixty-plus hours a week, serious problems will surface in your marriage, with your children, or with your physical or mental health. It's not a question of if, but *when.*

PASSIVE PROBLEM SOLVING

It is hard to be proactive without boundaries. People who don't stick to their boundaries will often act like the little Dutch boy who kept scurrying, helter-skelter, trying to halt leaks in the dyke by plugging his finger in one leak after another.

Rarely are people on the offense, *proactively* solving problems. Most operate on the defense, only *reacting* to pressures from various sources such as: scrambling to find a plumber for a major pipeline leak instead of repairing it before it reached crisis mode, or not arranging ahead of time for enough cars to carpool to a little league game.

Countless men and women rush from crisis to crisis, from panic to panic, trying to fix problems at work, at home, and elsewhere—all the while neglecting their own personal care time and family commitments.

I saw a cartoon that showed a man walking his dog on a leash, with the dog lifting its leg over a fire hydrant. The quote below the drawing, which I've paraphrased here, was priceless:

Ever feel like a fire hydrant, and everyone else is a dog, always using you to meet his own needs?

HUMAN ROBOTS

Many individuals eventually become emotionally-absent "human robots." They present a positive, outwardly successful shell that says, "I've got it all together," but they have no real life apart from their work.

This phenomenon doesn't happen only to working professionals. In a 2013 MTV interview, singer Miley Cyrus said, "There's no life for me other than entertaining."

Many people, if they are honest, might as well reword Miley's statement to say, "There's no life for me other than my job as a [doctor, computer programmer, mechanic, teacher, lawyer, business professional, architect, contractor . . .]."

I include myself in this "robot" category—my job was my whole life, with few hobbies, limited time for family, and an inadequate social life.

Can you identify with Miley and me? Is your whole life taken over by your work? Do you have a life *outside* of your career? Do you have any time or energy left after work to do personal or family activities? Because of the demands of your job, you may be tempted to emotionally detach from your family, preoccupying yourself only with things work-related—eventually becoming a human robot.

Keeping up a good front in a non-stop, fast-paced robotic life is exhausting. You feel totally drained—physically, emotionally, and spiritually—and your mental outlook and physical health deteriorates. Your gas tank runs on fumes. Your patience is thin, and your anger boils just below the surface.

To your loved ones, it seems as if "your lights are on, but no one's home." You are physically present, yet mentally and emotionally absent. Your spouse and kids may complain, but you defend yourself by saying, "It's just been an extra-busy week. After this week's over, things will slow down."

Such behavior can eventually become an addiction, a lifestyle you can't give up. By not adhering to boundaries and priorities, overworked people often find escape and comfort in a compulsive habit: emotionally detaching from family and friends, working longer hours, eating or drinking excessively, abusing legal or illegal drugs, taking sexual risks, or spending recklessly. This addictive, robotic behavior hurts a leader's ability to effectively manage a local business, non-profit organization, or family.

DAMAGED PERSONAL RELATIONSHIPS

A lack of boundaries can cause our relationships to suffer. I know of a father-daughter relationship that's still strained because of the father's unwillingness to set limits on his daughter's spending for her wedding. He simply said, "Get whatever you need." So she and her fiancé did just that.

They had a storybook wedding followed by a lavish reception. But the unlimited expense account later forced her father to work two jobs in an attempt to pay the wedding-related bills.

Not long after the wedding, his health failed due to his

long work hours and he had to file for bankruptcy. His lack of courage to set a "wedding-budget boundary" resulted in financial chaos and an unspoken damaged relationship with his daughter.

INEFFECTIVE WORK

Your effectiveness at work will suffer if you refuse to assign boundaries for professional and personal limits. The Bible cautions against excessive work hours, "*In vain you rise early and stay up late, toiling for food to eat.*" [1]

Although I knew this scriptural warning, for years I disregarded it, believing that I was different, that I could put in extra-long hours and still maintain a quality work and family life. Instead of arranging for adequate personal and family times, I sacrificed my own health for the sake of others. And once my personal health began to fail, I was not as able to effectively engage at work.

POOR SELF CARE

The Old Testament's King Solomon, apparently a workaholic, penned these words (paraphrased here) thousands of years ago, "*Why am I working like a dog and never having any fun?*" [2]

Fortunately, he was later able to pass on the things he learned about the importance of balance in his life. Like Solomon, I have tried to gain from my mistakes, sharing with others what I've learned through setting and maintaining boundaries.

Consider the following examples from two gifted women, Jan Dravecky and Jennifer Garner. They illustrate how our own problems with time management, relationships, and boundaries can add unnecessary burdens to our already busy lives.

Jan Dravecky is married to Dave Dravecky, a former major league baseball pitcher. Along with her numerous other responsibilities, Jan is a busy mom. A few years ago, she reflected on her addictive desire to be needed. Does the following quote from Jan sound familiar to you and your life?

> I was saying yes to my kids and yes to my husband and yes to my friends, but I rarely said yes to myself. My set of rules dictated that if a need existed, I needed to fill it. [3]

Actress Jennifer Garner, a mother of two young daughters, shared a similar sentiment, "I understood how to take care of people, but I didn't know how to ask for anything I needed. It was important to balance it out."

Do you often struggle with finding the balance between work, play, and self-nourishment? What are your biggest problem areas? How have poor boundaries affected your life?

CHAPTER 5

When to Create Boundaries

I KNEW A MAN IN FLORIDA WHO REPEATEDLY IGNORED HIS car's check-engine light. He kept driving, week after week, and finally the engine burned out. His failure to pay attention to the warning signs cost him nearly $2,000 in repairs.

Unfortunately, there is no quick, easy formula for balancing the demands of career, family, and personal time. But if you are starting to see your own internal "check-engine light" come on, then it may be time to consider making some changes with what you will and will not tolerate. You can consider this your "boundary-evaluating and boundary-setting challenge" for the month.

Consider these Bible verses as you reflect on and revise your boundary-toleration limits for your schedule and relationships:

The prudent give thought to their steps. [1]

Be very careful, then, how you live—not as unwise but as wise, making the most of every opportunity. [2]

There is a time for everything, and a season for every activity under heaven . . . a time to tear down and a time to build . . . a time to search and a time to give up, a time to keep and a time to throw away . . . a time to tear and a time to mend, a time to be silent and a time to speak. [3]

The prudent see danger and take refuge, but the simple keep going and pay the penalty. [4]

A good starting place to work on time management is to rethink how you can use boundaries to protect and make the most of your personal, family, and work time. Perhaps asking yourself some boundary-clarification questions like these might help:

- At home or work, am I feeling some kind of "ouch," such as anxiety, fear, anger, resentment, guilt, or pressure related to a specific person or situation?
- Do the ways I'm using my time and gifts match biblical priorities? Are my efforts the *best* use of my skills and time?
- What behaviors and words from others are acceptable or unacceptable to me? What will I tolerate or not tolerate from others, or even from myself?
- What activities or relationships should I add, drop, or change?
- What changes to my schedule and relationships will cause the least collateral damage?

Sometimes, setting boundaries and protecting them also means changing or eliminating them. Remember the lyrics to singer Kenny Rogers's hit song, "The Gambler"?

His words have profound boundary-setting implications for some activities and relationships at work, home, and elsewhere:

> Every gambler knows
> that the secret to survivin'
> is knowin' what to throw away
> and knowin' what to keep . . .
> You got to know when to hold 'em,
> know when to fold 'em,
> know when to walk away,
> and know when to run. [5]

There are times when a work project or even a family activity will need to be cut or temporarily suspended. These changes can sometimes result in harsh opposition, but they are often necessary for the long-term health of you, your family, and your job.

Remember Jesus's teaching about the necessity of pruning *fruit-bearing* trees? Consider his words, *"I am the true vine and my Father is the gardener . . . every branch that does bear fruit he prunes so that it will be* ***more*** *fruitful."* [6] He emphasized the importance of cutting back on *still-productive* trees so that they would produce even *more* fruit.

Though painful, pruning is often necessary for greater professional growth. Dr. James Dobson, a popular Christian author and psychologist, found this out when he set a time-use boundary that meant he had to stop teaching a very popular adult couples' Sunday school class that he and his wife had taught for years.

His decision ruffled a lot of feathers. However, if he had tried to please others by yielding to their expectations, he would have had less time to produce the books, articles, radio shows, and other media outreaches that have now reached tens of thousands of people.

When you prune your activities, at first it may seem like a bad decision. Other people may criticize you, and you might second-guess yourself. It may be difficult to believe that your decisions will result in more success at work or a more rewarding family and personal life. Initially, your pruning efforts might even result in inner havoc. But stick with it.

There could be certain relationships or work activities that pull you from your major career focus, personal plans, or family concerns. These "diversions" can take their toll—physically, emotionally, and spiritually. Setting specific boundaries on what work, church, or community meetings you'll skip will open time for more important things.

Sometimes pruning also needs to be done on your personal or family activities, not just your work schedule. Paul hints at this when he says, "*Let us purify ourselves from everything that contaminates body and spirit.*" [7]

By setting and following clear boundaries in your personal life, you will experience increased self-confidence and inner calm, less stress, better mental and physical health, and more enjoyable relationships.

In addition, your willingness to set boundaries and stick with them will bring you a clearer sense of who *you* are. You will gain a new sense of self-respect because your boundaries are a strong affirmation to yourself—that you are not an object to be trampled on, but rather a human being with dignity, who is entitled to respect and fair, humane treatment.

Despite some initial opposition, in the long term you'll receive *strong benefits* from setting clear "lines in the sand" and sticking to them. Your work will reap huge rewards and you'll gain credibility through increased effectiveness.

CHAPTER 6

Guidelines for Creating Clear Boundaries

HOW CAN YOU SET BOUNDARIES THAT WILL PROTECT AND enhance your job performance, family time, and personal life? Consider these seven suggested guidelines:

1. Redefine your concept of success.
2. Beware of the tyranny of the urgent.
3. Take better care of yourself.
4. Commit to taking better care of your family.
5. Identify passive or aggressive areas of conflict.
6. Write down your clear, measurable boundaries and share them with friends.
7. Revise, drop, or add boundaries as needed.

GUIDELINE 1: REDEFINE YOUR CONCEPT OF SUCCESS.

Do you measure your success in terms of salary, personal achievements, the reputation of your company or organization, the size of its membership, or its budget? Is your self-worth measured by your position or by what others say about you?

When these are your primary yardsticks, most of your time and efforts will be devoted to achieving these goals. You will probably have very little life outside of your career. If the success of your work is your *main* objective, then your marriage and parenting roles will take second place to your work tasks. The line between your work and family will blur, and compromises will happen.

You can choose to let your job consume your life. Or, maybe you can broaden your definition of success to include things other than just your work accomplishments. Maybe success can *also* include how well you perform as a spouse, parent, friend, bicyclist, jogger, fisherman, stamp collector, or neighbor. And if your view of success already includes these and other non-work categories, are you allotting sufficient blocks of time to them?

GUIDELINE 2: BEWARE OF THE TYRANNY OF THE URGENT.

Satan uses various methods to derail us from fulfilling God's plans. Writer Richard Foster noted that "in contemporary society our Adversary [Satan] majors in three things: noise, hurry, and crowds. If he can keep us engaged in 'muchness' and 'manyness,' he will rest satisfied." [1]

More than twenty-five years ago, Dr. Charles Hummel, President of Inter-Varsity Christian Fellowship, wrote a popular booklet titled *Tyranny of the Urgent!* [2] He explained that daily living will always be jammed with dozens of "urgent" demands on your time and energy: to-do lists, phone interruptions, paperwork, and other time-robbers. These smaller, less-important things eat up time, waste energy, and prevent us from focusing on our key priorities.

Oh, how I agree with Hummel. Like many of my colleagues, I've wrestled with "urgent" matters constantly pecking at my heels throughout my career.

The fact is that most of us don't actually need more

time—we need to *reprioritize* the time we have. The majority of time management experts agree that the key to maximizing time use is to do what is important first, and then move on to other tasks.

Several years ago, in the midst of fighting my way through an overwhelming list of "urgent" to-dos, I wrote a prayer to help me keep a healthy sense of perspective. I've had to read it out loud to myself countless times since then. I share it here so you can gain a revitalized perspective that might reduce your stress and increase your efficiency.

Here's a brief prayer for serenity in the midst of a busy, overloaded week:

> God, I just can't get it all done. I'm sick and tired of playing catch-up day after day, of scrambling at triple speed, and of working so many overtime hours. I quit! I need *your* help to survive emotionally. Only *you* can keep me from being overwhelmed by sheer panic, guilt, and resentment. Only *you* can guide and protect me. Please grant me *your* peace as I now surrender myself, my workload, and my self-destructive thoughts to *your* care and protection.

Note: A longer version of this prayer is included in the Appendix.

GUIDELINE 3: TAKE BETTER CARE OF YOURSELF.

In the book of Matthew, Jesus taught that one of the greatest commandments was, "*Love your neighbor as yourself.*" [3] But how can we love others if we don't first love ourselves?

Good self care will keep us healthy and prevent us from inadvertently harming others.

Sometimes You Have to Put Yourself First

Recall the last flight you took. Just before your plane took off, a flight attendant probably said, "If we encounter turbulence or oxygen-deprivation problems, the overhead oxygen masks above your seat will drop. Those of you with young children, please put the mask on yourself first, and then put one on your child." In other words, adults responsible for children must make sure their own oxygen supply is cared for first, in order to then help their child with oxygen. This reminds passengers that if they pass out due to a lack of oxygen, they cannot help their child, and both will suffer.

The same idea holds true for busy people—we frequently put the needs of others before our own. We do a good job of taking care of business tasks and people at work, but we only get average grades, at best, in nurturing our loved ones and ourselves. And we and our families often exist on the leftovers of our time and energy.

Have you ever heard the saying, "All work and no play makes Jack a dull boy"? After years of merely paying lip service to this saying, I now understand how absolutely necessary it is to have balance between work and play.

Oftentimes when I'd logged in too many hours of work for too many weeks in a row without any time off, I found myself resenting my schedule and getting impatient with people. After many years, I've found that pacing myself and taking time for hobbies, exercise, and other non-church activities has made a huge difference—in my personal, family, and church life.

Personal Care Boundaries

English playwright and poet William Shakespeare pointed out this tendency to continually give, while seldom addressing personal needs, when he penned this line in *The Life of King Henry V*: "Self-love, my liege, is not so vile a sin as *self-neglecting*." (emphasis added)

Maybe this is one of the reasons the Apostle Paul urged the leaders of the Ephesian church: "*Keep watch over* ***yourselves*** *and all the flock of which the Holy Spirit has made you overseers.*" [4]

Good self care means making time for a spiritually-nourishing inner life, reading, exercising, eating wisely, sleeping enough, practicing a hobby, and taking a full day off each week. This may also mean applying some new time boundaries, which will include disciplining your schedule to allow for things like:

- walking three hours a week with an exercise partner;
- taking a complete day off every week, and if something interrupts that day, making it up within a month;
- seeing a therapist for counseling; or
- scheduling several hours a week to enjoy a hobby.

GUIDELINE 4: COMMIT TO TAKING BETTER CARE OF YOUR FAMILY.

God knows we're vulnerable to neglecting ourselves and our families' needs, so he warns us, "*If anyone does not provide for his relatives, and especially for his household, he has denied the faith and is worse than an unbeliever.*" [5]

Providing a house, food, clothing, and schooling is important for taking care of your family's physical needs.

But equally important is meeting their emotional, spiritual, and mental needs—not only in quality of time but also in quantity of time. What, specifically, can you do to develop better balance between work, family, and yourself?

Marriage Strengthening Boundaries

Perhaps showing better care for your spouse may mean saving fifteen minutes every evening after dinner so the two of you can share your highs and lows of the day. It might include making time to have weekly half-day dates with your spouse. Or, you could make it happen by arranging your schedule to take your spouse away, without the kids, for a two-day "mini-moon" a few times a year.

Parenting Boundaries

Maybe following through on having better child-nurturing boundaries could mean taking each child out for a two-hour "date" each week. It could also include scheduling time every year to take each child on a weekend adventure, such as hiking, fishing, camping, or traveling.

GUIDELINE 5: IDENTIFY PASSIVE OR AGGRESSIVE AREAS OF CONFLICT.

Ask yourself, "What's causing my inner discomfort?" Usually your inner wincing is caused by toxic people or situations.

People-caused "hurts" can come from coworkers, employees, family, friends, church or organization members, and other sources.

Situation-caused "hurts" can come from things like relationships at work, job assignments, church people and programs, community obligations, social events, and family happenings.

GUIDELINE 6: WRITE DOWN YOUR CLEAR, MEASURABLE BOUNDARIES AND SHARE THEM WITH FRIENDS.

Veteran boundary-setters offer two tips for making and communicating clear, measurable boundaries.

First, *be specific* in setting your boundaries. Your specifics could include measurable boundaries like:

- I will stop attending a weekly non-priority meeting so that I can join a weight-loss group.
- I will cut out five appointments each month, and I will use this time to take up tennis and watercolor painting.
- I will guard my time by setting my cell phone's alarm to ring after having met with someone for fifty minutes.
- I will take the home phone off the hook from 5:30 to 7:30 every evening to ensure uninterrupted rest and family time.

Second, *communicate* your boundaries clearly, firmly, and gently by speaking or writing to those who might be affected. Explain what actions and words you *will* and *will not* permit. Additionally, share these boundaries with a few safe friends so that they can hold you accountable if you're tempted to give in to others' demands.

GUIDELINE 7: REVISE, DROP, OR ADD BOUNDARIES AS NEEDED.

Sports teams have timeouts and halftimes to evaluate how their strategies are doing and update their game plans. Likewise, you should periodically monitor how well your boundaries are working.

To evaluate the success of my boundaries, I ask myself a few questions:

- Have I written down the specific, measurable boundaries I want to achieve?
- Have I discussed my boundaries and their effectiveness with a friend who can give me balanced feedback?
- How successful have these boundaries been? Would I grade them with an A, B, C, D, or F?
- Have I spoken up when someone has tried to disrespect a boundary?
- Am I willing to flex, tighten, drop, or set new boundary limits?

How about asking yourself these same questions?

CHAPTER 7

Strategies to Protect Your Boundaries

IN BOXING, RIGHT BEFORE THE FIGHT STARTS, THE REFEREE motions the fighters to the center of the ring and gives last minute instructions to them, including the warning: "Protect yourselves at all times." This is wise advice for anyone, not just professional boxers.

Think about it: police wear SWAT vests, and football players use helmets and shoulder pads to protect themselves from injury. As laypersons, we must look after our own needs and protect ourselves from the hurtful words and behaviors of others. Instead of SWAT vests or shoulder pads, we use boundaries to emotionally and mentally safeguard ourselves and the people we care for.

Here are ten battle-tested strategies to better enforce your boundaries:

1. Expect both external and internal opposition.
2. Meet regularly with safe, supportive friends.
3. "Bookend" to protect yourself.
4. Refuse to argue with your critics.
5. Don't take criticisms personally.
6. Leave toxic, accusatory people as soon as possible.
7. Make it a habit to say no at least once a day until you become comfortable setting boundaries.

8. Use the "Secret Three-Word Formula" instead of giving in to others.
9. Say the full Serenity Prayer when under stress.
10. Forgive yourself and others.

STRATEGY 1: EXPECT BOTH EXTERNAL AND INTERNAL OPPOSITION.

When you follow through on your boundary limits, you'll almost always encounter confrontation, criticism, and conflict. As you create and implement boundaries, think through who will be offended. Robert Frost's poem "Mending Wall" deals with this reality. One phrase reads:

> Before I built a wall, I'd ask to know
> What I was walling in or walling out,
> And to whom I was like to give offense. [1]

External opposition will be the most obvious. You have chosen to take a stand, so don't be surprised when you face resistance. Expect to be treated negatively and hit by zinging words or looks from people who don't like your boundaries.

They may try to shame, blame, slander, punish, or avoid you. Or, they may simply disregard and bulldoze over your boundaries.

Poet E. E. Cummings writes about this kind of external opposition:

> In a world which is doing its best,
> night and day,
> to make you everybody else—
> means to fight the hardest battle

which any human being can fight;
and never stop fighting. [2]

I recently had firsthand experience with external opposition from a friend with whom I played golf every Monday morning.

I woke up with a terrible cold and a high temperature on the morning of our game. Having gone through pneumonia twice in the past five years, I didn't want to risk my cold getting more serious.

I called and cancelled, explaining my health issues. His response startled me—he did everything he could to talk me *into* playing. He joked, shamed, and rationalized, trying to get me to join him.

To stand firm on my "no" boundary, I had to battle both his outward pressure and my internal stress (which was created by the worry that I had been a wimp in letting a sniffle stop my golf game).

This story reveals that you can also anticipate *internal* resistance from your own thinking, emotions, and self-talk. Be prepared to deal with inner feelings of guilt, fear, anger, regret, and even depression as you set and hold on to your boundaries.

For example, let's say that you have an overbearing mother who insists you come for dinner every Thursday night. You finally tell her that you only have time to come over one night a month. She immediately shoots that hurting, dagger stare that says, "After all I've done for you, how could you treat me this way?"

Her words start your internal opposition. You begin saying to yourself, "Yes, I guess I am a selfish, self-centered, ungrateful son who only comes to dinner with his mother once a month." Then your emotions seesaw between guilt for disappointing your mother, and resentment for having her dictate another area of your life.

STRATEGY 2: MEET REGULARLY WITH SAFE, SUPPORTIVE FRIENDS.

In *The Friendless American Male*, a book that came out over thirty years ago, author David W. Smith revealed that the vast majority of American men do not have a single male friend whom they can call to discuss serious personal problems. Since then, that alarming truth has been validated by dozens of studies.

If you are a male reader, does *The Friendless American Male* describe you? Can you say, "I think I can call at least one friend at 2:00 a.m., and I wouldn't have to apologize for asking for any type of help, whether it's something practical, prayer, or just to be there for me during my time of need"?

A good friend listens and validates concerns; helps to process raw feelings of anger, fear, and frustration; adds a balanced perspective; and gives guidance. An anonymous writer noted, "If you have even one close friend in life, you are most blessed." Consider this statement from the Bible:

> *Two are better than one, because they have a good return for their labor. If one falls down, his friend can help him up. But pity the man who falls and has no one to help him up! Also, if two lie down together, they will keep warm. But how can one keep warm alone? Though one may be overpowered, two can defend themselves.* [3]

Do you have one or two special friends with whom you can share anything, anytime, and anywhere? If not, think about cultivating some relationships to see if one or two might end up being a safe, trustworthy, and uplifting counselor.

STRATEGY 3: "BOOKEND" TO PROTECT YOURSELF.

"Bookending" is contacting someone before and after you go into a potentially stressful situation. I use this technique often and have found it to be extremely helpful, especially when confronting boundary issues. Before you go into a potentially stressful situation, call a friend to explain your concerns and ask for her prayers. Then, as soon as you leave, call that person again and share what happened—the positives and negatives.

While the Bible encourages us to rely on God for help, it also urges us to lean on others for helpful support:

> *Let us consider how we may spur one another on toward love and good deeds, not giving up meeting together, as some are in the habit of doing, but let us encourage one another.* [4]

Those in Alcoholics Anonymous and other 12-step groups use this "bookending" strategy frequently and with great success. How about trying it yourself?

STRATEGY 4: REFUSE TO ARGUE WITH YOUR CRITICS.

Remain calm and firm as you describe your boundaries. If you say something like, "I've decided to not take phone calls, emails, or texts over mealtimes because I need to set aside that time for my family," expect that some people will be hurt, even offended, by your mealtime limits.

The reality is that there will *always* be someone who doesn't agree with the reasons for your boundaries. It's a waste of time to go into lengthy justifications for your decisions. The Bible explains, "*Do not speak to fools, for they will scorn your prudent words.*" [5] Even if you offer a gentle, reasonable explanation, some folks will be upset or even trample on your boundaries. Therefore, it's often easiest to simply state your new limits and trust that God will protect you.

STRATEGY 5: DON'T TAKE CRITICISMS PERSONALLY.

One of life's tough realities is that whenever anyone attempts to be successful at something, there will always be critics. Come up with a new product, service, program, or boundary and you will inevitably clash with a few naysayers.

Keep in mind that 90 percent of the time your critics' adverse comments represent their own problems, not yours. Antagonistic responses often come from someone who is threatened, jealous, or fearful of the effects of your newly set limits.

When someone makes negative comments about your new boundary, ask yourself, "What's going on in this person's work or family life? What's his motive for attacking me? What does he stand to gain if I don't enforce this new boundary?" This thought exercise will change your perspective and help you realize that not all criticism is a result of *your* actions.

STRATEGY 6: LEAVE TOXIC, ACCUSATORY PEOPLE AS SOON AS POSSIBLE.

Those who stay in a hostile environment will often cave in and agree with their accusers. Or, they will start beating themselves for being so "pig-headed" in making such "awful" perimeters. Remaining in the presence of negative, cutting people can inflict painful emotional wounds on you. You will become a human punching bag, with others beating you with their words.

Consider the Bible's wisdom from Proverbs: "*Do not make friends with a hot-tempered person, do not associate with one easily angered, or you may learn their ways and get yourself ensnared.*" [6]

What can you do in these circumstances? Either leave the room or ask the hurtful person to leave.

STRATEGY 7: MAKE IT A HABIT TO SAY NO AT LEAST ONCE A DAY UNTIL YOU BECOME COMFORTABLE SETTING BOUNDARIES.

Think of the last time you resumed exercising after a lengthy rest. You probably used some muscles that hadn't been active for a long time—remember how sore you were for the next few days? The same thing happens when you've not been accustomed to setting and maintaining boundaries. It can be painful when you begin to exercise your long-dormant "no" boundary muscles, so begin with fairly safe areas:

- Say no to eating when you're not hungry.
- Say no to a request to attend a social event you don't want to attend.

- Say no to a friend who wants you to run an errand with him when what you really want is to stay home and play with your kids or watch a TV show.
- Say no to your inner voice that nags, "Before you go home, you've got to finish *all* your work and return every phone call *right now*."

STRATEGY 8: USE THE "SECRET THREE-WORD FORMULA" INSTEAD OF GIVING IN TO OTHERS.

When confronted with a boundary issue, counter it by using the phrase: "Love to, can't." Your conversation might go like this, filling in the details as needed:

> I'd love to [do what you're asking] . . . Sorry, I can't [because I have another commitment].

Don't waste time defending your decision—forgo any explanations. This will save you the turmoil of having to justify your actions, yield to others' expectations, or shame yourself for your decision.

Concentrate on using the Formula to protect yourself from being pressured into undesirable stresses. These could include things like social, family, work, or church commitments. They also could include new, unwanted tasks or responsibilities.

STRATEGY 9: SAY THE FULL SERENITY PRAYER WHEN UNDER STRESS.

Perhaps best known for its use in 12-step programs, the Serenity Prayer is a valuable spiritual tool for anyone, not just for recovering alcoholics and other addicts.

Most people are only aware of the traditional, shorter version that includes just the first few words of this famous prayer (attributed to Dr. Reinhold Niebuhr). Its complete version is even more helpful, and I highly recommend using it. I, and countless others, have used this powerful prayer to gain stability and guidance in turbulent times.

Serenity Prayer (Complete Version)

God, grant me serenity to accept the things I cannot change, courage to change the things I can, and wisdom to know the difference; living one day at a time, enjoying one moment at a time; accepting hardship as a pathway to peace; taking, as Jesus did, this sinful world as it is, not as I would have it; trusting that you will make all things right if I surrender to your will, so that I may be reasonably happy in this life and supremely happy with you in the next. Amen.

STRATEGY 10: FORGIVE YOURSELF AND OTHERS.

It's easy to let your life be weighed down by your own or others' harmful words or actions. If you've failed to set adequate boundaries and you and others have suffered, admit it to God. He graciously offers *complete* forgiveness no matter how badly you've botched up.

If others have hurt you in any way, forgive them, but don't trust that they won't repeat their offenses. Don't put yourself in harm's way again. Learn from people's patterns and from your own pain, then choose to move ahead.

Sometimes, forgiving and moving ahead are exceedingly hard—while forgiveness starts with a decision to try to forgive, it frequently takes a long time to process wounds, sometimes months or even years.

For instance, if you've been emotionally, physically, or sexually abused, it will take significant time to process your injuries and forgive others so that you can heal, rebuild, and forge ahead. As you undergo the process of healing, you'll find it easier to let go and move on.

REVIEWING KEY POINTS

BEFORE WE CONCLUDE, LET'S REVIEW THE KEY POINTS WE'VE considered about boundaries:

- According to experts, boundary issues are one of the toughest problems people face.
- A boundary is "any line or thing marking a limit." Boundaries are not goals. They are limits—barriers used to protect, improve, or enhance goals.
- Boundaries play key roles in the Bible.
- There are different kinds of boundaries, but most are physical or emotional in nature. They show what words and behaviors you *will* and *will not* accept from others.
- A vast number of people live with no boundaries, or the ones they do have are weak, vague, or unenforced, which results in negative individual, relational, and work consequences.
- Key boundary areas are: relationships with certain family members, relatives, and other people; work; personal finances; social obligations; and the expectations others have of you.
- Some common boundary-related stresses are: violations of phone-call boundaries at meal times, verbal abuse, interruptions of evenings and days off, job description issues, and infringements of personal limits.
- Surviving and thriving in your occupation, home, and personal life require ongoing boundary setting,

monitoring, and enforcing. Doing this will result in great benefits but, at times, stiff opposition.

- Sometimes it's necessary to cut out certain activities or relationships in order for greater benefits to occur.
- The timing of *when* to set boundaries is important.

Fellow boundary-strugglers recommend these guidelines for *setting* boundaries:

1. Redefine your concept of success.
2. Beware of the tyranny of the urgent.
3. Take better care of yourself.
4. Commit to taking better care of your family.
5. Identify passive or aggressive areas of conflict.
6. Write down your clear, measurable boundaries and share them with friends.
7. Revise, add, or let go of your boundaries.

Lastly, let's look again at the top battle-tested boundary *protection* strategies:

1. Expect both external and internal opposition.
2. Meet regularly with safe, supportive friends.
3. "Bookend" to protect yourself.
4. Refuse to argue with your critics.
5. Don't take criticisms personally.
6. Leave toxic, accusatory people as soon as possible.
7. Make it a habit to say no at least once a day until you become comfortable setting boundaries.

8. Use the "Secret Three-Word Formula" instead of giving in to others.
9. Say the full Serenity Prayer when under stress.
10. Forgive yourself and others.

These suggestions have helped me and many others protect our boundaries. Try applying and adapting them to your unique situation.

CONCLUSION

WHEN CONSISTENTLY APPLIED, THE THINGS WE'VE DISCUSSED in this book will help relieve many of your boundary tensions. You now know specific boundary ideas you can use to protect and improve your career, your family, and your personal life.

Pat yourself on the back for having the courage to look at your own boundary issues and for investing time to learn better ways to rein in unnecessary stresses. Putting into practice good boundary controls will be an adventure that will pay big dividends for you, your family, and your vocation!

I hope that as you experiment with setting and maintaining boundaries, you will experience what Robert Frost wrote in his famous poem "The Road Not Taken":

> Two roads diverged in a yellow wood,
> And sorry I could not travel both
> And be one traveler, long I stood
> And looked down one as far as I could
> To where it bent in the undergrowth;
>
> Then took the other, as just as fair,
> And having perhaps the better claim,
> Because it was grassy and wanted wear;
> Though as for that the passing there
> Had worn them really about the same,

And both that morning equally lay
In leaves no step had trodden black.
Oh, I kept the first for another day!
Yet knowing how way leads on to way,
I doubted if I should ever come back.

I shall be telling this with a sigh
Somewhere ages and ages hence:
Two roads diverged in a wood, and I—
I took the one less traveled by,
And that has made all the difference. [1]

Our conversation about boundaries has barely scratched the surface, but we've covered the basics. Now it's up to you to work out how these tips will apply to your life. You will become your own boundary expert.

As you begin, or continue, your boundary efforts, may God continue to bless you, your family, and your work.

ACKNOWLEDGMENTS

I SINCERELY APPRECIATE THE FOLLOWING PEOPLE FOR THEIR help in making this book happen:

My psychologists, who counseled and taught me about boundaries and helped me to clarify, strengthen, and maintain them: Phil Sutherland, John Townsend, Henry Cloud, Maribeth Ekey, and Laurel Basbas. They were key in counseling, consoling, and guiding me as I set, reset, and worked to maintain healthy personal and professional boundaries.

My editors, who gave valuable shaping and guidance in manuscript details: Andrew Kroeger and Stephanie Starr.

My copyeditors and proofreaders, who corrected grammar and typographic flaws: Shelley Atwood, Sharon Young, Janelle Killingsworth, Daniel Skadal, and Elijah Dove.

My office helpers, who copied, collated, stapled, and filed articles used in the research and production of this book: Stephen Reese, Lisa Waldschmidt, Becky Trinklein, and Robert Langdale.

My computer technicians, who installed programs, fixed computer glitches, and taught me, the ultimate computer-challenged writer, how to survive in a techie world and not lose my faith in the process: Taylor Allee and Mike Adler.

My permissions researchers: Sean Fernald, Susan Lessick, and Rebecca Trinklein.

My typist, who saved me much time and untold typos: Lyssa Eschel.

My friends, who listened to my struggles and successes: Dan Ardell, Lucky and Penny Arnold, Connie Bean, Larry and Sue Ann Beaty, John Chandler, Dr. Gunnar and Susan Christiansen, Gex Coons, Dr. Dick and June Cooper, Dick and Cathy Dowell, Ed Egloff, Ellen Enochs, Jeff Fryer, Fred and Joan Hearn, Ron and Catherine Hilliard, Cliff Ishigaki, Bob and Joan Johnson, Dr. Gregory Katz, Jack and May Kline, Jim Kok, Bill and Annie Lightcap, Bob and Marilyn Long, Scott and Carolyn McOwen, Bob Numrich, Ozzie and Cleo Purdy, Vince Roman, Dr. Himasiri De Silva, Ken Stokes, Jake and Alice Swartout, Tom Taillon, Bill and Chris Tassio, Scott and Patti Thompson, Hank and Margaret Weber, and others.

And above all, the God of Scripture, who patiently put up with my boundary botches, and sent people and information my way to educate, rehabilitate, and encourage me in my boundary journey.

APPENDIX

Time Management Prayer

GOD, PLEASE HELP ME TO SEE THAT THE ESCALATING VOLUME of work tasks, family responsibilities, and social obligations are *ongoing* pressures, rather than urgent emergencies. Give me *your* perspective on them. Empower me with the grace to do my best, leaving the results, complete and incomplete, up to your control.

Open my mind to accept that a workday ought to be eight to ten working hours, that a workweek should be five or, at most, six days a week, and that every week I must have at least one clean day off. Help me to see this as a reasonable, balanced, wise, and healthy schedule.

Deliver me from my fear-based, pride-driven workaholism. Spare me from resenting my work. Save me from self-recriminations for the unfinished items on my to-do list. Rescue me from the inner upset of facing yet another day of nearly impossible-to-complete projects.

The Bible says, "*He grants sleep to those he loves.*" [1] Oh, how I need your peaceful rest, so that tonight I might not, again, experience a sleepless night, torn by restless anxieties over tomorrow's tasks.

Slow me down from wearing myself out trying to please people. Free me from my feverish addiction to placating others, and from slavery to their opinions of my work. Grant me the courage to endure the hurt of disappointing some when I cut back or leave certain things unfinished. Strengthen me to withstand others' views that my accomplishments aren't good enough.

Help me to truly accept the reality that no matter what I do or don't do, it will always rub some the wrong way, that I will never please everyone, and that I will never complete in a day, a week, a month, or a year, all the assignments, calls, letters, emails, texts, appointments, and meetings that come my way. Enable me to do my best and then truly accept that "all I can do is all I can do."

This is the day which you have made. I will rejoice that you, not I, are in charge of it. *You* are the Director of the play—I accept that I am merely a small member of your cast.

Open my eyes today to the little things you send my way to alert me of your presence. Help me to be grateful for your blessings of yesterday, and your beautiful world around me right now.

Sensitize me to obey the nudges of your spirit. Guide me now in focusing on applying the slogans: "Easy does it," "Keep it simple," "First things first," "One day at a time," and "Let go and let God." Help me to prioritize, cut out, add to, or change today's tasks.

As an act of faith, I turn myself and all my work, family, and other to-dos over to you, trusting that you will continue to care for and protect me from others' negative responses and my own self-condemnations. I now drop all my work-related worries, fears, and resentments into your strong arms and surrender to your guidance.

I am yours, O Lord. Send me. Use me. I ask these things in the name of Jesus Christ, my Friend, Strength, Guide, and Savior. Amen.

NOTES

CHAPTER 1

1. Numbers 34:1–2, 12
2. Luke 5:15–16

CHAPTER 2

1. *Webster's New World College Dictionary.*

CHAPTER 3

1. *The Poetry of Robert Frost*, excerpt from the poem "Stopping by Woods on a Snowy Evening"

CHAPTER 4

1. Psalms 127:2
2. Ecclesiastes 4:8 (The Message)
3. Jan Dravecky, endurance.org.

CHAPTER 5

1. Proverbs 14:15
2. Ephesians 5:15–16
3. Ecclesiastes 3:1, 3, 6–7
4. Proverbs 22:3
5. "The Gambler", written by Don Schlitz
6. John 15:1-2 (emphasis added)
7. 2 Corinthians 7:1

CHAPTER 6

1. *Celebration of Discipline: The Path to Spiritual Growth*, by Richard J. Foster
2. "Tyranny of the Urgent", by Dr. Charles Hummel
3. Matthew 22:39
4. Acts 20:28 (emphasis added)
5. 1 Timothy 5:8

CHAPTER 7

1. *The Poetry of Robert Frost,* excerpt from the poem "Mending Wall"
2. Excerpt from *A Poet's Advice to Students.* Cummings
3. Ecclesiastes 4:9–12
4. Hebrews 10:24–25
5. Proverbs 23:9
6. Proverbs 22:24–25

CLOSING THOUGHTS

1. *The Poetry of Robert Frost,* "The Road Not Taken"

APPENDIX

1. Psalms 127:2

PERMISSIONS

I sincerely appreciate permissions granted to me to include excerpts from the following publications:

ABOUT THE AUTHOR

Rev. Dr. Jim Stout is an ordained Presbyterian minister who has pastored in five churches. His other ministry experiences include working with college and graduate students at Harvard, MIT, Boston, Northeastern, and Miami universities; doing social work with Young Life's outreach to teenage gangs in New York City; and working as student chaplain to the men's violent ward at Danvers Massachusetts State Mental Hospital.

He was given the National Alliance for the Mentally Ill (NAMI) California's "Distinguished Clergy Award" for his efforts on behalf of those affected by mental illness.

In college, he participated in varsity football and wrestling, and won Golden Gloves heavyweight boxing championships in Pennsylvania and Ohio. Since then, he has competed in triathlons and finished seven- and eight-day group rides on his bike.

He received his Master of Divinity from Gordon-Conwell Theological Seminary and his Doctor of Ministry from Fuller Theological Seminary.

He has been married to the former Leah Ann Hayden since 1967. They have two sons, Jim Jr. and John, and four energetic grandchildren.

HAS THIS BOOK BEEN HELPFUL?

If this book has been helpful to you, please give it a review and share it with others.

A quick, honest review on Amazon (it takes less than a minute) will help others discover the book. I'd love to hear your stories of how this book has helped you, and your feedback will help me improve this book and many future writing projects.

Consider gifting copies to people who might also benefit. But first, please listen carefully to their pain and add your own supportive words of strength, hope, and experience.

Would you like to schedule an interview or speaking engagement?

Please contact me through my website, www.drjimstout.com. Unfortunately, my schedule does not permit personal counseling.

Want to stay up-to-date with my new books and articles?

To join my author list for new articles, behind-the-scenes looks at upcoming books, and book giveaways, please sign up at www.drjimstout.com/join. As a thank you for joining, I'll send you a FREE digital copy of my personal testimony book, *Recovering and Rebuilding from a Severe Mental Illness.*